Fisherman Crochet Afghans

Designs by Anne Rabun Ough

TABLE OF CONTENTS

Maumelle. Arkansas ● Leisure Arts, Inc.

Approx Finished Size: 45" x 65" each

#1 Limerick Afghan

Photo shown on page 2.

Materials: Approx 56 oz (1590 gr) Worsted Wt yarn
Crochet hooks sizes I (5.5 mm) **and** J (6 mm)
or sizes needed for gauge

Gauge: In sc, 3 sts = 1", 3 rows = 1"

Size: Approx 45" x 65"

Pattern Stitches Used: Low Ridge Front, Low Ridge Back, Cable, Shadow Box, Bow Tie and Woven Stitch.

NOTE: Before beginning to work, it will be helpful to familiarize yourself with the pattern stitches used by making a 6" swatch and working through each pattern.

Woven Stitch pattern may require a larger size hook in order to keep gauge equal to other stitches. If the sides of the swatch are not even, change to larger size hook on Woven Stitch rows throughout afghan.

INSTRUCTIONS

Row 1: With smaller size hook, ch 214; sc in 3rd sc from hook and in each ch across; ch 1, turn: 212 sc.

Row 2: Sc in next sc ***(Fig. 7a, page 13)*** and in each sc across, ending by working sc in turning ch ***(Fig. 7b, page 13)***; ch 1, turn.

Rows 3 and 4: Work Low Ridge Front ***(abbreviated LRF) (Figs. 9a&b and photo, page 13)*** patt Rows 1 and 2.

Rows 5 and 6: Work Cable ***(Figs. 14a-d and photo, page 15)*** patt Rows 1 and 2, ending Row 6 by working 2 sc in turning ch: 70 cables.

Rows 7 and 8: Rep Rows 3 and 4 (LRF).

Rows 9 and 10: Rep Row 2, twice; at end of Row 10, ch 2, turn.

Row 11 (Shadow Box): With **right** side facing, dc in next sc, ★ skip next 2 sc, work tr in each of next 2 sc, working **behind** tr just worked, tr in each of 2 skipped sc, skip next 2 sc, tr in each of next 2 sc, working in **front** of 2 tr just worked, tr in each of 2 skipped sc, dc in each of next 2 sc; rep from ★ across, ending by working last dc in turning ch; ch 2, turn.

Row 12: Dc in next dc, ★ skip next 2 tr, tr in each of next 2 tr, working **behind** tr just worked, tr in each of 2 skipped tr, skip next 2 tr, tr in each of next 2 tr, working in **front** of tr just worked, tr in each skipped tr, dc in each of next 2 dc; rep from ★ across; ch 1, turn: 21 Boxes.

SHADOW BOX – multiple of 10 plus 1 st, 2 rows.

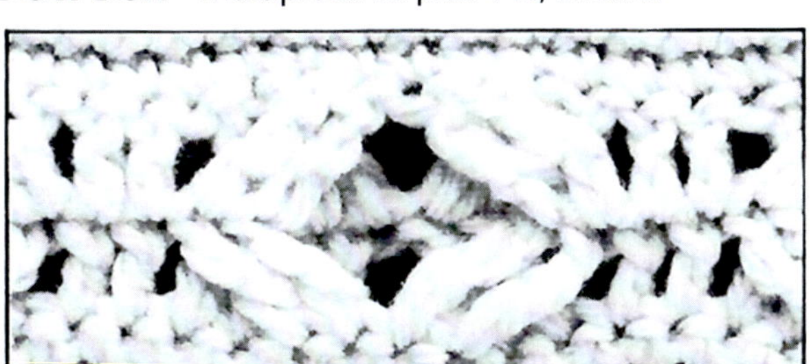

Row 13: Sc in next st and in each st across; ch 1, turn.

Rows 14 and 15: Rep Row 2, twice.

Row 16 (Low Ridge Back) *(abbreviated LRB)*: With **wrong** side facing, working in **back loop only *(abbreviated BLO) (Fig. 8, page 13)***, sl st in next sc and in each sc across, ending by working sl st in turning ch; ch 1, turn.

Row 17: Working in unused lp of Row 15, sc in first sc ***(Fig. 1)*** and in each sc across; ch 2, turn.

LOW RIDGE BACK *(abbreviated LRB)* – worked on any number of sts, 2 rows.

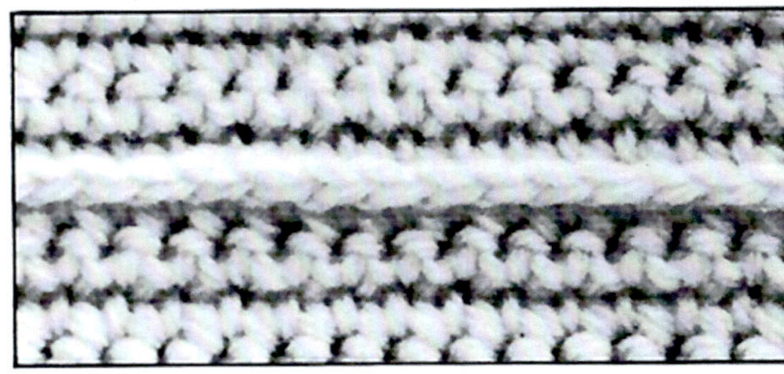

Fig. 1

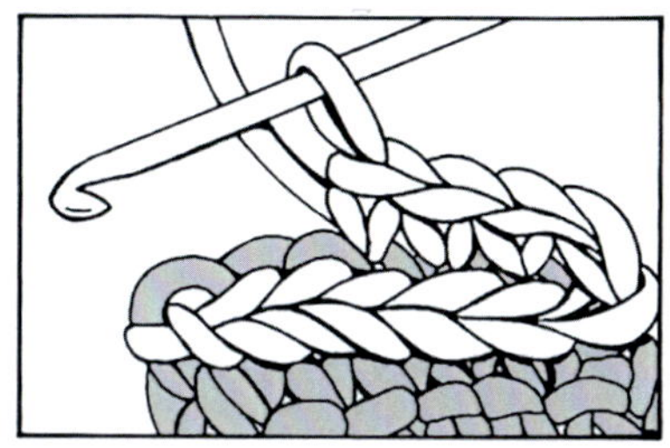

Row 18 (Woven Stitch) *(abbreviated WS)*: Change to larger size hook, skip first sc, YO, insert hook in next sc, hook yarn and pull up through stitch and one lp on hook, hook yarn and pull through 2 lps on hook ***(Fig. 2a, page 4)*** (1 lp rem on hook); **first half of WS made**: YO, insert hook in same sc, hook yarn and in one continuous motion pull yarn through stitch and both lps on hook ***(Fig. 2b, page 4)*** (1 lp rem on hook); **2nd half of WS made *(Fig. 2c, page 4)***, ★ skip next sc, work WS in next sc; rep from ★ across; ch 2, turn: 106 WS.

WOVEN STITCH *(abbreviated WS)* – multiple of 2 sts, 1 row.

Fig. 2a

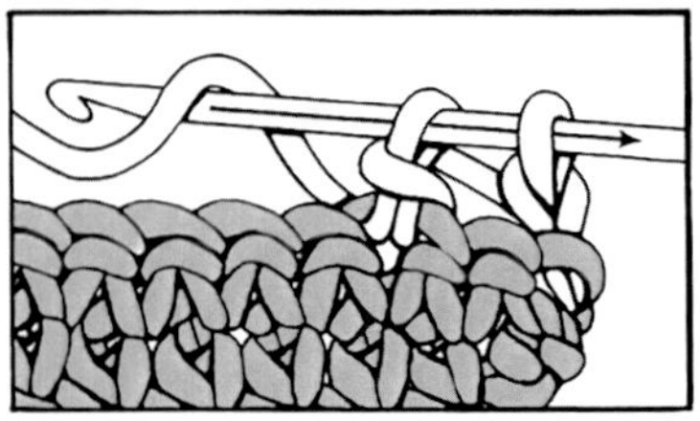

Fig. 2b

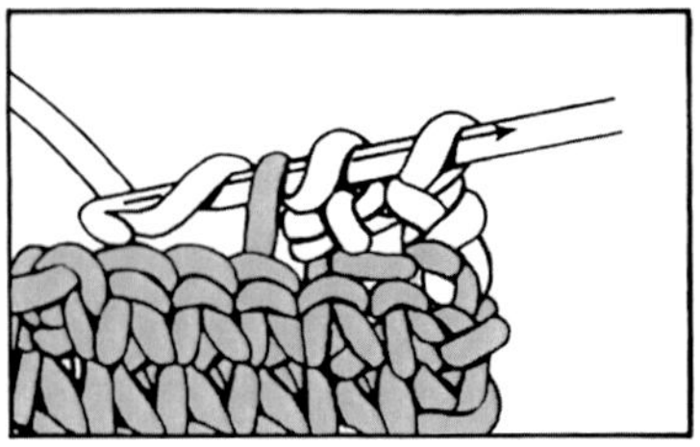

Fig. 2c

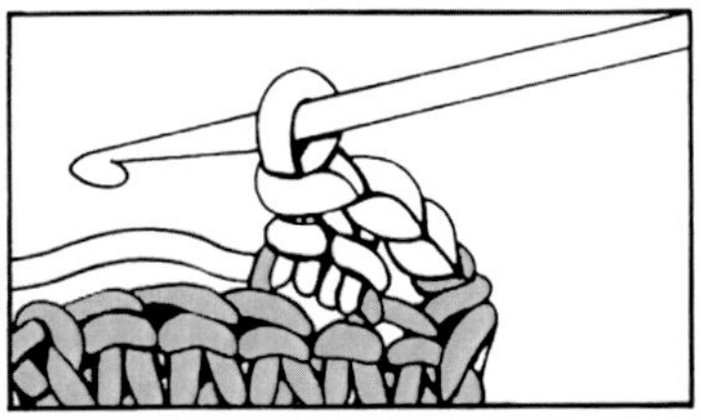

Row 19: Work WS in each sp between WS of prev row, ending by working last WS in turning ch; ch 2, turn.

Rows 20-36: Rep Row 19, 17 times **more**; at end of Row 36, ch 1, turn: 19 rows WS.

Row 37: Work 2 sc in each sp between WS across, ending by working 2 sc in turning ch; ch 1, turn.

Rows 38 and 39: Change to smaller size hook, rep Rows 16 and 17 (LRB).

Rows 40 and 41: Rep Row 2, twice.

Row 42 (Bow Tie): ***(Note:*** Bow Tie is same as Shadow Box, but worked from the **wrong** side.) With **wrong** side facing, rep Row 11.

Row 43: With **right** side facing, rep Row 12 **(Bow Tie completed)**: 21 Bow Ties.

BOW TIE - same as Shadow Box on reverse side.

Row 44: Rep Row 13.

Rows 45 and 46: Rep Row 2, twice.

Rows 47 and 48: Rep Rows 3 and 4 (LRF).

Rows 49-61: Change to larger size hook, rep Rows 18-30 (13 rows Woven Stitch).

Row 62: Rep Row 37 (finishing row of Woven Stitch).

Rows 63-68: Change to smaller size hook, rep Rows 3-8 (LRF, Cable, LRF).

Rows 69-74: Rep Rows 9-14 (Shadow Box).

Rows 75-80: Rep Rows 3-8 (LRF, Cable, LRF). (***Note:*** Be sure to change to larger size hook for WS rows.)

Rows 81-94: Rep Rows 49-62.

Rows 95 and 96: Rep Rows 3 and 4 (LRF).

Rows 97-99: Rep Row 2, 3 times.

Rows 100-102: Rep Rows 42-44 (Bow Tie).

Rows 103-129: Rep Rows 15-41 (LRB, WS, LRB).

Rows 130-134: Rep Rows 10-14 (Shadow Box).

Rows 135-140: Rep Rows 3-8; at end of Row 140, ch 1, turn; do **not** finish off.

Finishing: Sl st in first sc and in each sc across last row, ch 1, rotate piece to work across end, sc in end of last row, ★ ch 1, skip next row, sc in end of next row; rep from ★ across end, adjusting as necessary to keep edge flat; ch 1, working into unused lp of beg ch, complete other side and end in same manner, ending by working sl st in beg sl st; finish off.

Work Triple Lattice Fringe ***(Fig. 5 and photo, page 12)*** on each end.

#2 Armagh Afghan

Photo shown on page 2.

Materials: Approx 60 oz (1704 gr) Worsted Wt yarn
Crochet hook size I (5.5 mm) **or** size needed for gauge

Gauge: In sc, 3 sts = 1", 3 rows = 1"

Size: Approx 45" x 65"

Pattern Stitches Used: Knurl, Arrow, Low Ridge Front, High Ridge Front, Cable, Diamond, Fishbone and Popcorn Diamond.

NOTE: Before beginning to work, it will be helpful to familiarize yourself with the pattern stitches used by making a 6" swatch and working through each pattern.

INSTRUCTIONS

Row 1: Ch 196, sc in 3rd ch from hook and in each ch across; ch 1, turn **(now and throughout)**: 194 sc.

Row 2: Sc in next sc ***(Fig. 7a, page 13)*** and in each sc across, ending by working sc in turning ch ***(Fig. 7b, page 13)***.

Rows 3 and 4: Work High Ridge Front ***(abbreviated HRF) (Fig. 10 and photo, page 13)*** patt Rows 1 and 2.

Rows 5 and 6: Work Cable ***(Figs. 14a-d and photo, page 15)*** patt Rows 1 and 2: 64 cables.

Rows 7 and 8: Work Low Ridge Front ***(abbreviated LRF)*** patt Rows 1 and 2 ***(Figs. 9a&b and photo, page 13)***; at end of Row 8, ch 3, turn.

Row 9 (Arrow): Dc in next sc, ★ skip next 3 sc, tr in next sc, working **behind** tr just worked, dc in each of 3 skipped sc; rep from ★ across, ending by working dc in turning ch; ch 3, turn.

Row 10: ★ Skip next 3 dc, tr in next tr, working in **front** of tr just worked, dc in each of 3 skipped dc; rep from ★ across, ending by working dc in last dc and in turning ch; ch 1, turn.

ARROW – multiple of 4 plus 2 sts, 2 rows.

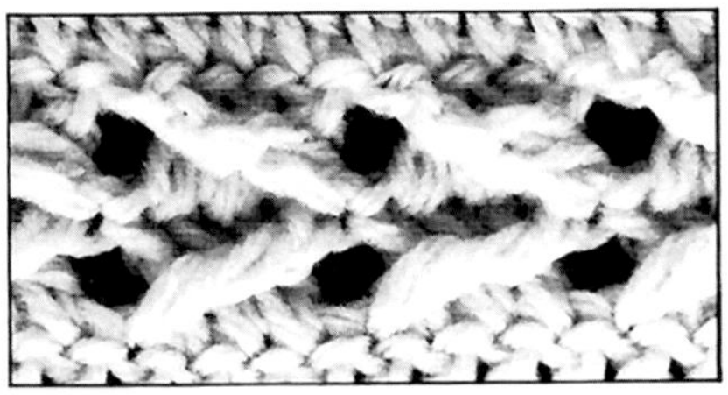

Row 11: Sc in next st and in each st across, ending by working sc in turning ch; ch 1, turn.

Row 12: Rep Row 2.

Rows 13 and 14: Rep Rows 7 and 8 (LRF).

Rows 15 and 16: Rep Rows 5 and 6 (Cable).

Rows 17 and 18: Rep Rows 7 and 8 (LRF).

Row 19: Rep Row 2.

Rows 20-22 (begin Diamond): Work Diamond ***(photo, page 14)*** patt Rows 1-3.

Row 23: Work Diamond patt Row 4, ending by working sc in each of last 4 sc; ch 1, turn.

Rows 24-26: Rep Rows 20-22.

Row 27 (end Diamond): Work Diamond patt Row 8, ending by working tr around sc next to last tr, skip next sc, sc in each of last 2 sc; ch 1, turn: 32 Diamonds.

Rows 28-35: Rep Rows 20-27.

Rows 36-38: Rep Row 11, 3 times.

Rows 39-44: Rep Rows 13-18 (LRF, Cable, LRF).

Rows 45 and 46: Rep Row 2, twice; at end of Row 46, ch 3, turn.

Row 47 (Fishbone): Dc in next sc, ★ skip next 2 sc, tr in each of next 2 sc, working in **front** of 2 tr just worked, tr in each of skipped 2 sc, dc in next 2 sc; rep from ★ across, ending by working dc in turning ch; ch 1, turn.

Row 48: Working in **back loop only *(abbreviated BLO) (Fig. 8, page 13)***, sc in each st across, ending by working sc in turning ch; ch 2, turn.

Row 49: Working in each unused lp of Row 47, skip first lp, dc in next dc, ★ skip next 2 tr, tr in each of next 2 tr, working **behind** 2 tr just made, tr in each of 2 skipped tr, dc in each of next 2 dc; rep from ★ across, ending by working dc in turning ch; ch 1, turn.

FISHBONE – multiple of 6 plus 1 st, 4 rows.

Row 50: Sc in next st and in each st across, ending by working sc in turning ch; ch 1, turn.

Rows 51 and 52: Rep Row 2, twice.

Rows 53 and 54: Rep Rows 3 and 4 (HRF).

Rows 55-58: Work Knurl ***(Figs. 11a-d and photos, pages 13 & 14)*** patt Rows 1-4.

Rows 59 and 60: Rep Rows 3 and 4 (HRF).

Rows 61 and 62: Rep Row 2, twice.

Rows 63-72: Work Popcorn Diamond ***(photo, page 15)*** patt Rows 1-10.

Rows 73-84: Rep Rows 51-62 (HRF, Knurl, HRF).

Rows 85-94: Rep Rows 63-72 (Popcorn Diamond).

Rows 95-106: Rep Rows 51-62; at end of Row 106, ch 3, turn (HRF, Knurl, HRF).

Rows 107-110: Rep Rows 47-50 (Fishbone).

Rows 111-144: Rep Rows 11-44.

Rows 145-148: Rep Rows 9-12 (Arrow).

Rows 149 and 150: Rep Rows 7 and 8 (LRF).

Rows 151 and 152: Rep Rows 5 and 6 (Cable).

Rows 153 and 154: Rep Rows 3 and 4 (HRF).

Row 155: Rep Row 2; ch 1, do **not** turn.

Finishing: Working through both lps of last row from **left** to **right**, † work Knurl patt Row 2 across; ch 1, turn to work across end, with **wrong** side facing, sc in end of last row, ★ ch 1, skip next row, sc in end of next row; rep from ★ across end, adjusting as necessary to keep edge flat; † ch 1, with **right** side facing and working Knurl Stitch into unused lp of beg ch, rep from † to † across beg side and other end, ending by working sl st in beg st of border; finish off.

Work Tied Fringe ***(Fig. 6 and photo, page 12)*** on each end.

3
4
Approx
Finished Size:
45" x 65" each

#3 Londonderry Afghan

Photo shown on page 6.

Materials: Approx 61 oz (1732 gr) Worsted Wt yarn
Crochet hooks sizes I (5.5 mm) **and** J (6 mm)
or sizes needed for gauge

Gauge: In sc, 3 sts = 1", 3 rows = 1"

Size: Approx 47" x 65"

Pattern Stitches Used: Fisherman Popcorn, Low Ridge Front, Popcorn Diamond and Knurl.

NOTE: Before beginning to work, it will be helpful to familiarize yourself with the pattern stitches used by making a 6" swatch and working through each pattern. The Fisherman Popcorn pattern may require a larger size hook in order to keep gauge equal to other stitches. If pattern rows pull in at edges, use a larger size hook for these rows.

INSTRUCTIONS

Row 1: With smaller size hook, ch 196, sc in 3rd ch from hook and in each ch across; ch 1, turn **(now and throughout)**: 194 sc.

Row 2: Sc in next *sc* ***(Fig. 7a, page 13)*** and in each sc across, ending by working sc in turning ch ***(Fig. 7b, page 13)***.

Row 3: Rep Row 2.

Rows 4 and 5: Work Low Ridge Front ***(abbreviated LRF) (Figs. 9a&b and photo, page 13)***.

Row 6: Change to larger size hook, work Fisherman Popcorn patt Row 1 ***(photo, page 14)***: 48 Popcorns.

Row 7: Work 2 sc in each ch-1 sp, ending by working 2 sc in turning ch: 194 sc.

Rows 8 and 9: Change to smaller size hook, rep Rows 4 and 5 (LRF).

Rows 10-13: Work Knurl patt Rows 1-4 ***(Figs. 11a-d and photo, pages 13 & 14)***.

Rows 14 and 15: Rep Rows 4 and 5 (LRF).

Rows 16 and 17: Rep Row 2, twice.

Rows 18-27: Work Popcorn Diamond patt Rows 1-10 ***(photo, page 15)***: 24 PC Diamonds.

Rows 28 and 29: Rep Row 2, twice.

Rows 30-51: Rep Rows 8-29.

Rows 52-59: Rep Rows 8-15 (LRF, Knurl, LRF).

Row 60: Change to larger size hook, rep Row 6.

Rows 61-64: Work Fisherman Popcorn patt Rows 2-5.

Rows 65-110: Rep Rows 61-64, 11 times **more**, then rep Rows 61 and 62 once.

Row 111: Rep Row 7: 194 sc.

Rows 112-155: Change to smaller size hook, rep Rows 8-29, twice.

Rows 156-163: Rep Rows 8-15 (LRF, Knurl, LRF).

Rows 164-167: Rep Rows 6-9.

Rows 168 and 169: Rep Row 2, twice; at end of last row ch 1, turn.

Finishing: † Sl st in first st and in each st across, ch 1, rotate piece to work across short end, sc in end of last row, ★ ch 1, skip next row, sc in end of next row; rep from ★ across end, adjusting as necessary to keep edge flat †; ch 1, turn, working in each unused lp of beg ch, rep from † to †, ending by working sl st in beg sl st of border; finish off.

Work Tied Fringe ***(Fig. 6 and photo, page 12)*** on each end.

#4 Dublin Afghan

Photo shown on page 6.

Materials: Approx 74 oz (2102 gr) Worsted Wt yarn
Crochet hook size I (5.5 mm) **or** size needed for gauge

Gauge: In sc, 3 sts = 1", 3 rows = 1"

Size: Approx 45" x 65"

Pattern Stitches Used: High Ridge Front, Aran, Knurl and Basketweave.

NOTE: Before beginning to work, it will be helpful to familiarize yourself with the pattern stitches used by making a 6" swatch and working several repeats of each pattern to check gauge.

INSTRUCTIONS

Row 1: Ch 213, sc in 3rd ch from hook and in each ch across; ch 1, turn **(now and throughout)**: 211 sc.

Row 2: Sc in next sc ***(Fig. 7a, page 13)*** and in each sc across, ending by working sc in turning ch ***(Fig. 7b, page 13)***.

Rows 3 and 4: Work High Ridge Front ***(abbreviated HRF) (Fig. 10 and photo, page 13)*** patt Rows 1 and 2.

Rows 5-8: Work Knurl ***(Figs. 11a-d and photo, pages 13 & 14)*** patt Rows 1-4.

Row 9: (begin Aran Pattern): Working in **front loop only *(abbreviated FLO) (Fig. 8, page 13)*** of prev row, sc in next sc, ★ work 1 ch, insert hook into back ridge of ch just made, sc in ch **(Double Chain made, *abbreviated Dch) (Fig. 3)***, work 2 more Dch in same manner, skip next 2 sc, sc in FLO of next sc; rep from ★ across, ending by working sc in turning ch; ch 1, turn: 70 lps.

Fig. 3

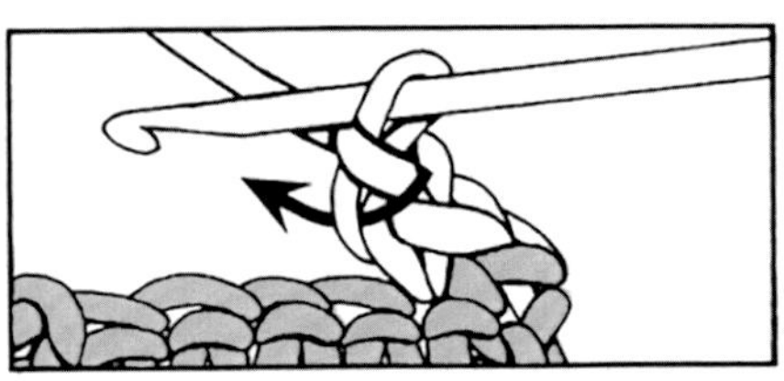

Row 10: Working through **both loops** of skipped sts and in each unused loop of prev row, sc in next sc and in each st across; ch 1, turn.

Rows 11 and 12: Sc in next sc and in each sc across, ending by working sc in turning ch; ch 1, turn.

Row 13: Working in FLO, sc in next sc, ★ work 1 Dch, sl st in 2nd Dch of first 3-Dch lp on Row 9, work 1 Dch, skip next 2 sc, sc in next sc; rep from ★ across, ending by working sc in turning ch; ch 1, turn.

Row 14 (end Aran): Rep Row 10.

ARAN STITCH - multiple of 3 plus 1 st, 6 rows.

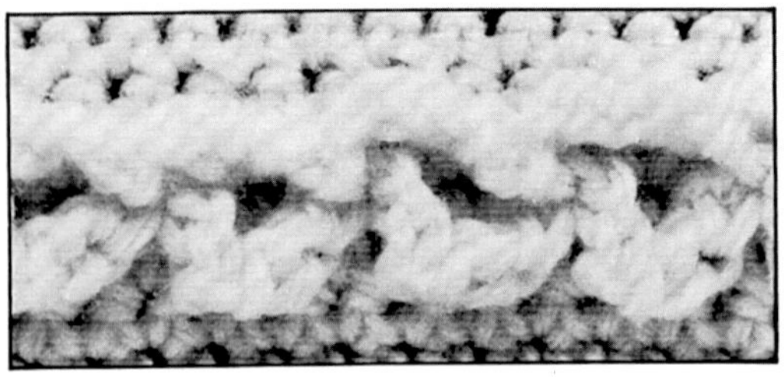

Rows 15-18: Rep Rows 5-8 (Knurl).

Rows 19 and 20: Rep Rows 3 and 4 (HRF); ch 2, turn.

Row 21 (begin Basketweave pattern): ★ Working from **back**, dc ***(abbreviated BPdc)*** around post of each of next 3 sc ***(Fig. 13, page 14)***, working from **front**, dc ***(abbreviated FPdc)*** around each of next 3 sc; rep from ★ across, ending by working hdc in turning ch; ch 2, turn.

Row 22: Working around dc post of prev row, ★ BPdc around each of next 3 sts, FPdc around each of next 3 sts; rep from ★ across, ending by working hdc in turning ch; ch 2, turn.

Row 23: Rep Row 22.

Row 24: ★ FPdc around each of next 3 dc, BPdc around each of next 3 dc; rep from ★ across, ending by working hdc in turning ch; ch 2, turn.

BASKETWEAVE - multiple of 6 plus 1 st, 6 rows.

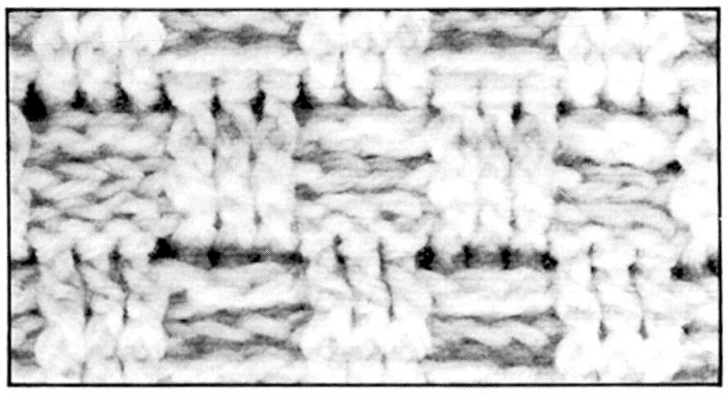

Rows 25 and 26 (end Basketweave): Rep Row 24, twice.

Rows 27-44: Rep Rows 21-26, 3 times **more**.

Rows 45-128: Rep Rows 3-44, twice **more**.

Rows 129-146: Rep Rows 3-20; at end of Row 146, ch 1, turn.

Row 147: Rep Row 2; at end of Row 147, ch 1, do **not** turn; do **not** finish off.

Finishing: † Working through both lps of prev row from **left** to **right,** work Knurl patt Row 2 across side; ch 1, turn to work along end with wrong side facing, sc in end of last row, ★ ch 1, skip next row, sc in end of next row; rep from ★ across end, adjusting as necessary to keep edge flat †; ch 1, with **right** side facing, working Knurl into unused lp of beg ch, rep from † to † across beg side and other end, ending by working sl st in beg st of border; finish off.

Work Triple Lattice Fringe ***(Fig. 5 and photo, page 12)*** on each end.

Approx Finished Size:
45" x 65" each

#5 Galway Afghan

Photo shown on page 9.

Materials: Approx 65 oz (1846 gr) Worsted Wt yarn
Crochet hooks sizes I (5.5 mm) **and** J (6 mm)
or sizes needed for gauge

Gauge: In sc, 3 sts = 1", 3 rows = 1"

Size: Approx 45" x 65"

Pattern Stitches Used: Low Ridge Front, Knurl, Fisheye and Fisherman Popcorn.

NOTE: Before beginning to work, it will be helpful to familiarize yourself with the pattern stitches used by making a 6" swatch and working through each pattern. The Fisherman Popcorn pattern usually requires a larger size hook to make gauge equal to other patterns. If Fisherman Popcorn pattern rows pull in at the edges, use a larger size hook for these rows.

INSTRUCTIONS

Row 1: With smaller size hook, ch 196, sc in 3rd ch from hook and in each ch across; ch 1, turn: 194 sc.

Row 2: Sc in next sc ***(Fig. 7a, page 13)*** and in each sc across, ending by working sc in turning ch ***(Fig. 7b, page 13)***; ch 1, turn.

Rows 3 and 4: Work Low Ridge Front ***(abbreviated LRF) (Figs. 9a-b and photo, page 13)*** patt Rows 1 and 2.

Rows 5-8: Work Knurl ***(Figs. 11a-d and photo, pages 13 & 14)*** patt Rows 1-4.

Rows 9 and 10: Rep Rows 3 and 4 (LRF).

Rows 11 and 12 (begin Fisheye): Rep Row 2, twice; at end of Row 12, ch 1, turn.

Row 13: Sc in each of next 2 sc, skip 5 sc on 3rd row **below** (Row 10), ★ tr in next sc, pull lp up to working row, finish tr, skip next sc on top row (Row 12), sc in each of next 3 sc, tr in same st on 3rd row **below** (Row 10) ***(Fig. 4)*** where last tr was made, skip next sc on Row 12, sc in each of next 3 sc, skip next 7 sc on Row 10; rep from ★ across, ending by working sc in last 2 sc and in turning ch; ch 1, turn.

Fig. 4

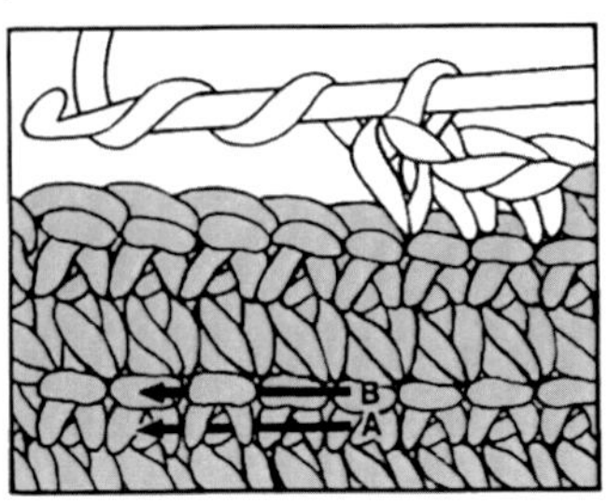

Row 14: Sc in next st and in each st across, ending by working sc in turning ch; ch 1, turn.

Row 15: ★ Sc in next sc, dc from **front** to **back** ***(Fig. 13, page 14)*** around first tr of Row 13, skip next sc on Row 14, sc in each of next 2 sc, work Popcorn ***(abbreviated PC) (Fig. 12, page 14)*** in next sc, sc in each of next 2 sc, dc around next tr of Row 13, skip next sc on Row 14; rep from ★ across, ending by working sc in last sc and in turning ch; ch 1, turn.

Row 16: Rep Row 14.

Row 17: Sc in each of next 2 sc, ★ dc around next dc of Row 15, skip next sc on Row 16, sc in each of next 3 sc, dc around next dc of Row 15, skip next sc on Row 16, sc in each of next 3 sc; rep from ★ across, ending by working sc in each of next 2 sc and in turning ch; ch 1, turn.

Row 18: Rep Row 14.

Row 19 (end Fisheye): Sc in each of next 4 sc, ★ (YO, insert hook around **next** dc, pull up yarn, YO, pull through 2 lps) twice, YO and pull through 3 lps, skip next sc on Row 18, sc in each of next 7 sc; rep from ★ across, ending by working sc in each of last 4 sc and in turning ch; ch 1, turn.

FISHEYE - multiple of 8 plus 2 sts, 9 rows.

Row 20: Rep Row 14.

Rows 21-28: Rep Rows 3-10 (LRF, Knurl, LRF).

Row 29: Change to larger size hook, work Fisherman Popcorn ***(abbreviated FPC) (photo, page 14)*** patt Row 1: 48 PC.

Rows 30-33: Work FPC patt Rows 2-5: 49 PC in Row 31 and alternate rows.

Rows 34-41: Rep Rows 30-33, 2 times **more:** 7 PC rows.

Row 42: Work 2 sc in each ch-1 sp across, ending by working 2 sc in turning ch; ch 1, turn.

Rows 43-68: Change to smaller size hook, rep Rows 3-28.

Row 69: Rep Row 29.

Rows 70-109: Rep Rows 30-33, 10 times **more:** 21 PC rows in **center panel**.

Row 110: Rep Row 42.

Rows 111-176: Rep Rows 3-68, changing hooks as before.

Row 177: Rep Row 2; ch 1, do **not** finish off.

Finishing: Working through both lps of last row from **left** to **right**, † work Knurl patt Row 2 across; ch 1, turn to work across end with **wrong** side facing, sc in end of last row, ★ ch 1, skip next row, sc in end of next row; rep from ★ across end, adjusting as necessary to keep edge flat †; ch 1, with **right** side facing, working Knurl into unused lp of beg ch, rep from † to † across beg side and other end, ending by working sl st in beg st of border; finish off.

Work Triple Lattice Fringe ***(Fig. 5 and photo, page 12)*** on each end.

#6 Cork Afghan

Photo shown on page 9.

Materials: Approx 66 oz (1874 gr) Worsted Wt yarn
Crochet hooks sizes I (5.5 mm) **and** J (6 mm)
or sizes needed for gauge

Gauge: In sc, 3 sts = 1", 3 rows = 1"

Size: Approx 47" x 65"

Pattern Stitches Used: Low Ridge Front, Cable, Knurl, Fisherman Popcorn and Diamond.

NOTE: Before beginning to work, it will be helpful to familiarize yourself with the pattern stitches used by making a 6" swatch and working through each pattern. The Fisherman Popcorn pattern usually requires a larger size hook to make gauge equal to other patterns. If Fisherman Popcorn pattern rows pull in at the edges, use a larger size hook for these rows.

INSTRUCTIONS

Row 1: With smaller size hook, ch 196, sc in 3rd ch from hook and in each ch across; ch 1, turn: 194 sc.

Row 2 and 3: Sc in next sc ***(Fig. 7a, page 13)*** and in each sc across, ending by working sc in turning ch ***(Fig. 7b, page 13)***; ch 1, turn.

Rows 4 and 5: Work Low Ridge Front ***(abbreviated LRF) (Figs. 9&b and photo, page 13)***.

Rows 6 and 7: Work Cable patt ***(Figs. 14a-d and photo, page 15)*** across: 64 cables.

Rows 8 and 9: Rep Rows 4 and 5 (LRF).

Rows 10-16 (begin Diamond): Work Diamond ***(photo, page 14)***, patt Rows 2-8, using Row 9 (last row of LRF) as first row of patt: 32 Diamonds.

Row 17: Sc in next st and in each st across, ending by working sc in turning ch; ch 1, turn.

Row 18-49: Repeat Rows 10-17, 4 times **more**: 5 rows of Diamonds.

Rows 50-55: Rep Rows 4-9 (LRF, Cable, LRF).

Rows 56-59: Work Knurl ***(Figs. 11a-d and photo, pages 13 & 14)*** patt Rows 1-4.

Rows 60-65: Rep Rows 4-9 (LRF, Cable, LRF).

Row 66: Change to larger size hook, work Fisherman Popcorn ***(photo, page 14)*** patt Row 1: 48 Popcorns ***(abbreviated PC)***.

Row 67: Work Fisherman Popcorn patt Row 2.

Row 68: Work Fisherman Popcorn patt Row 3: 49 PC.

Rows 69 and 70: Work Fisherman Popcorn patt Rows 4 and 5.

Rows 71-106: Rep Rows 67-70, 9 times **more**: 21 rows PC.

Row 107: Work 2 sc in each ch-1 sp across, ending by working 2 sc in turning ch; ch 1, turn.

Rows 108-123: Change to smaller size hook, rep Rows 50-65.

Rows 124-163: Rep Rows 10-49 (Diamond).

Rows 164-169: Rep Rows 4-9 (LRF, Cable, LRF).

Rows 170-172: Rep Row 2, 3 times; at end of last row, ch 1, turn.

Finishing: † Sl st in first sc and in each sc across, ch 1, rotating piece to work across end, sc in end of last row, ★ ch 1, skip next row, sc in end of next row; rep from ★ across end, adjusting as necessary to keep edge flat †; ch 1, turn to work in each unused lp of beg ch; rep from † to † once to complete other side and end, ending with sl st in beg sl st; finish off.

Work Tied Fringe ***(Fig. 6 and photo, page 12)*** on each end.

GENERAL INSTRUCTIONS

Fisherman Crochet offers a challenge to those who have not tried it. However, you will find that the patterns are made up of stitches you already know, worked in different techniques to become unique patterns. The distinctive characteristic of Fisherman Crochet is the texture formed on the right side, leaving the wrong side with the appearance of solid single crochet.

Try to master one new stitch at a time by following the instructions and referring to photographs, before working it into your afghan. You'll find the practice time well spent.

ABBREVIATIONS

approx	approximately	patt	pattern
beg	beginning	PC	popcorn
BLO	back loop only	prev	previous
ch(s)	chain(s)	rem	remain(s)(ing)
dc	double crochet	rep	repeat
Dch	double chain	sc	single crochet
est	established	sl st(s)	slip stitch(es)
FLO	front loop only	sp(s)	space(s)
gr	gram(s)	st (s)	stitch(es)
HRF	high ridge front	tr	treble crochet
LRB	low ridge back	tog	together
LRF	low ridge front	WS	woven stitch
lp(s)	loop(s)	wt	weight
oz	ounces	YO	yarn over

★ – work instructions following ★ as many **more** times as indicated in addition to the first time.

( ) – work enclosed instructions as many times as specified by the number immediately following or work all enclosed instructions in the stitch or space indicated.

† to † – work all instructions from first † to second † as many times as specified by the number immediately following.

GAUGE

Correct gauge is essential for proper sizing, and is extremely important in working Fisherman Crochet Afghans, since each pattern may have a slightly different gauge. A slight variation in gauge will be multiplied and much more evident over a greater number of stitches. For instance, if you have 3½ stitches per inch instead of 3, your finished afghan will measure only 55" long instead of 65", a difference of 10". Hook size given is merely a guide and should not be used without making a swatch. Before beginning to work, make a sample swatch in the hook and yarn and patterns to be used in your afghan, making the swatch large enough to measure at least 6" to determine gauge. Measure the single crochet rows for standard gauge. If some rows are shorter or longer than others, over the same number of stitches, change to a larger or smaller size hook for these rows. Keep trying until you find the size hook that will give you an even edge throughout all the patterns used in the afghan. We have found that the Woven Stitch pattern, when repeated over several rows, requires a larger size hook.

FRINGE

TRIPLE LATTICE FRINGE

Row 1: With afghan right side facing, join yarn in first sc at end, work 1 ch, insert hook in back ridge of ch just made ***(Fig. 1)***, sc in ch **(Double Chain made) (abbreviated Dch).** Work 2 more Dch in same manner, ★ sc in next ch-1 sp, work 3 Dch, skip next ch-1 sp; rep from ★ across, ending by working sc in last sc; turn.

Fig. 5

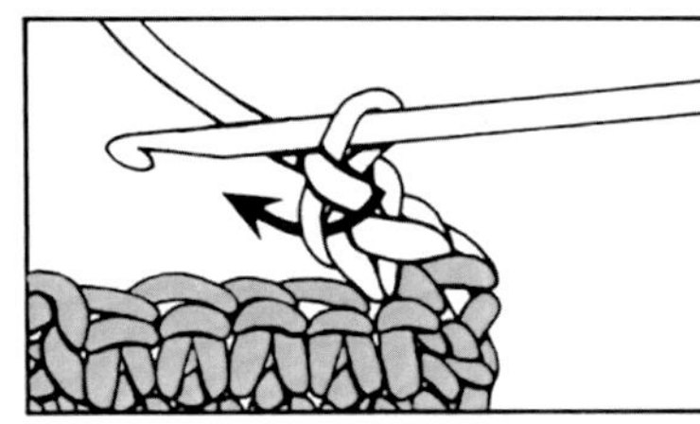

Row 2: ★ Work 3 Dch, sc in middle of next 3-Dch sp; rep from ★ across; turn.

Row 3: Rep Row 2; finish off.

Cut yarn in 16" strands. Using 5 strands tog, fold in half and with afghan wrong side facing, pull lp through 3-Dch sp, pull ends through lp and tighten knot ***(Fig. 6)***; rep across end. Work other end in same manner, cutting more strands as needed.

Fig. 6

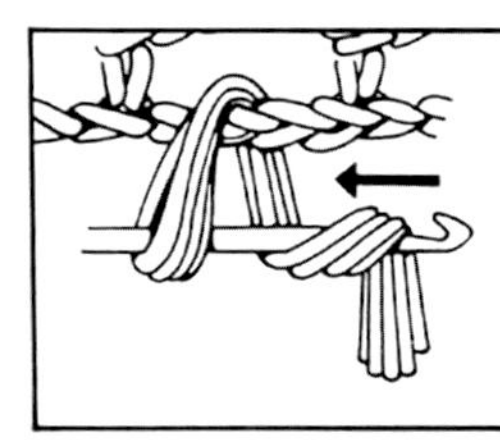

TIED FRINGE

Cut yarn in 20" strands. Using 5 strands tog, fold in half and with afghan wrong side facing, pull lp through ch-1 sp, pull ends through and tighten knot ***(Fig. 6)***; working in every other ch-1 sp, rep across end. Using all of outside group and half of next group, ★ tie in overhand knot about 1" down from prev knot, with rem strands and half of next group; rep from ★ across, tying all of last group in same manner as first.

Work other end in same manner, cutting more strands as needed.

PATTERN STITCHES

Pattern is worked into a foundation row of single crochet, which may be the ending row of the previous pattern.

The afghan is worked lengthwise in one piece, with a slip stitch or Knurl stitch border along the sides. Fringe is added to a chain stitch foundation worked on each end.

> To keep edges even at the end of each row, work **first stitch** into second loop ***(Fig. 7a)*** and **last stitch** into turning chain ***(Fig. 7b)*** of previous row unless otherwise instructed. Be sure to count stitches often to avoid "losing" a stitch.

Fig. 7a

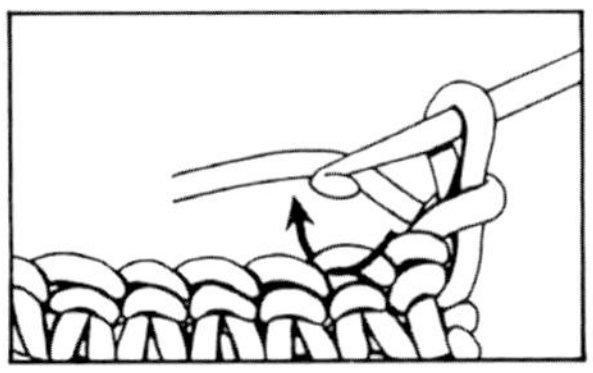

Fig. 7b

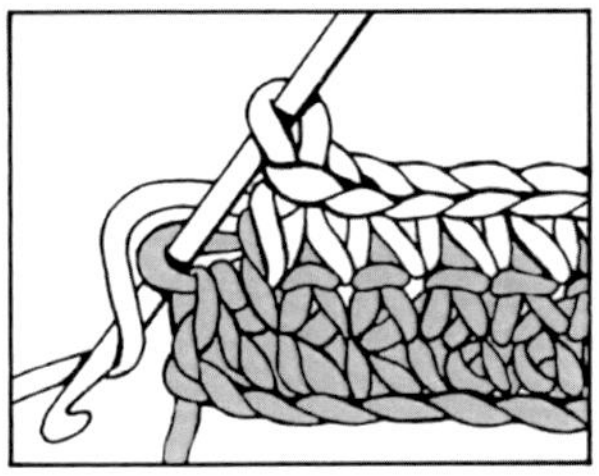

Photographs illustrate finished pattern rows, some of which are made up of combinations of familiar crochet stitches. Techniques unique to Fisherman crochet are described below with number of stitches required for pattern repeat.

LOW RIDGE FRONT *(abbreviated LRF)* – worked on any number of stitches, 2 rows.

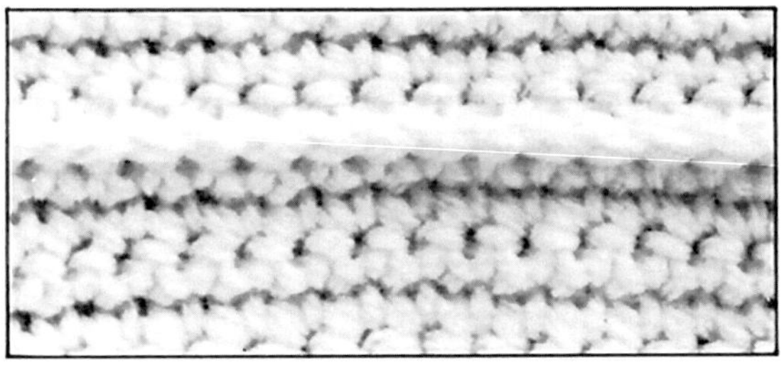

Row 1: With **right** side facing and working in **front loop only *(abbreviated FLO) (Fig. 8)*** of prev row, sl st in next sc and in each sc across ***(Fig. 9a)***, ending by working sl st in turning ch; ch 1, turn.

Fig. 8

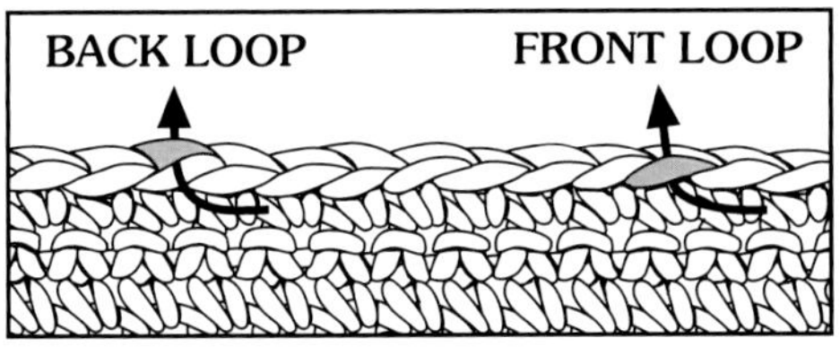

Row 2: Working in unused loop of prev row, sc in first sc and in each sc across ***(Fig. 9b)***; ch 1, turn.

Fig. 9a

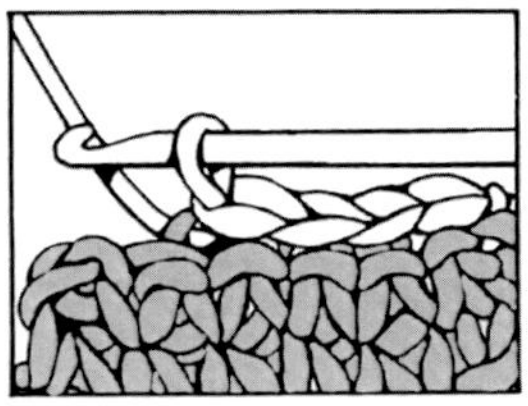

Fig. 9b

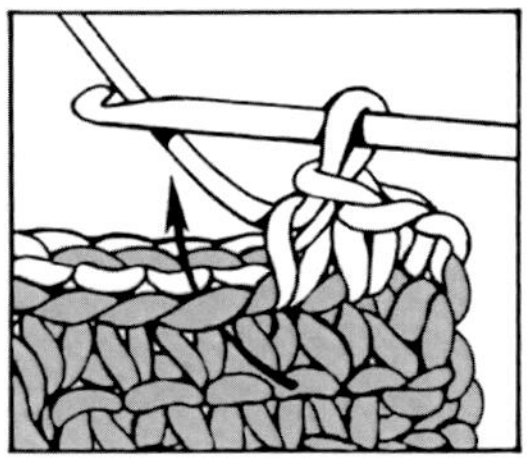

HIGH RIDGE FRONT *(abbreviated HRF)* – worked on any number of stitches, 2 rows.

Row 1: With **right** side facing and working in **front loop only *(abbreviated FLO) (Fig. 8)*** of prev row, sc in next sc and in each sc across, ending by working sc in turning ch; ch 1, turn.

Row 2: Working in unused loop of prev row, sc in next sc and in each sc across ***(Fig. 10)***, ending by working sc in turning ch; ch 1, turn.

Fig. 10

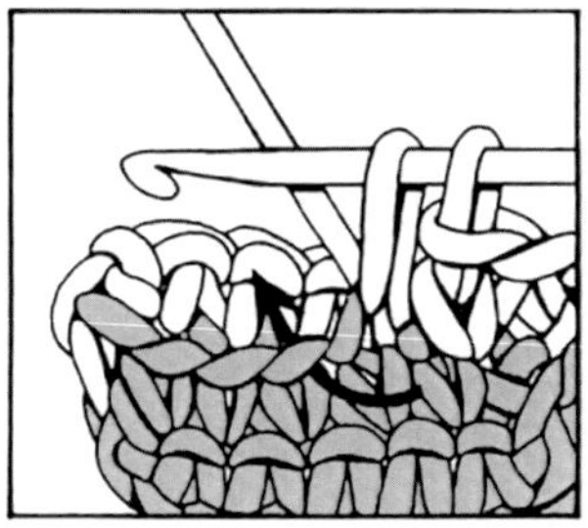

KNURL STITCH – worked on any number of stitches, 4 rows.

Row 1: Sc in next sc and in each sc across, ending by working sc in turning ch; ch 1, do **not** turn.

Note: Next row is worked from **left** to **right**; keep hook to left of work.

Row 2: Working in **front loop only *(abbreviated FLO) (Fig. 8, page 13)***, ★ insert hook in stitch to right of hook ***(Fig. 11a)***, hook yarn and draw through under and to left of loop on hook ***(Fig. 11b)*** (2 loops on hook), YO and draw yarn through both loops on hook ***(Fig. 11c)* (Knurl st completed) *(Fig. 11d)***; rep from ★ across, ending by working last st in turning ch; ch 1, do not turn.

Fig. 11a

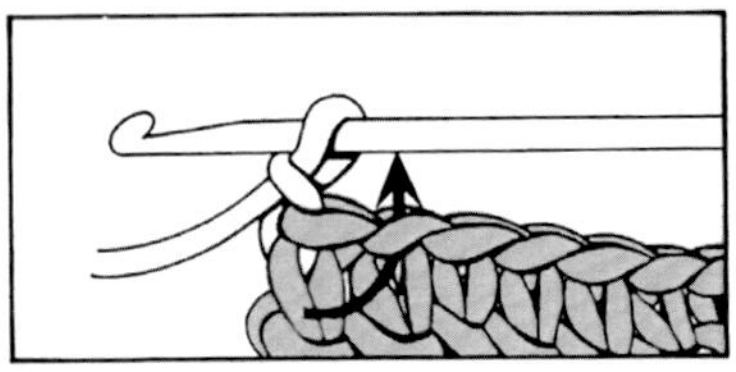

Fig. 11b

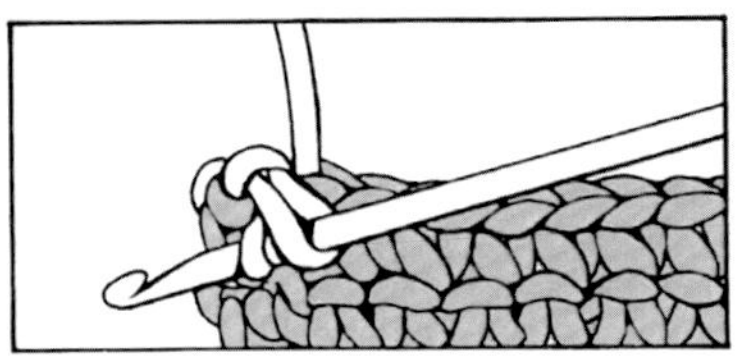

Fig. 11c

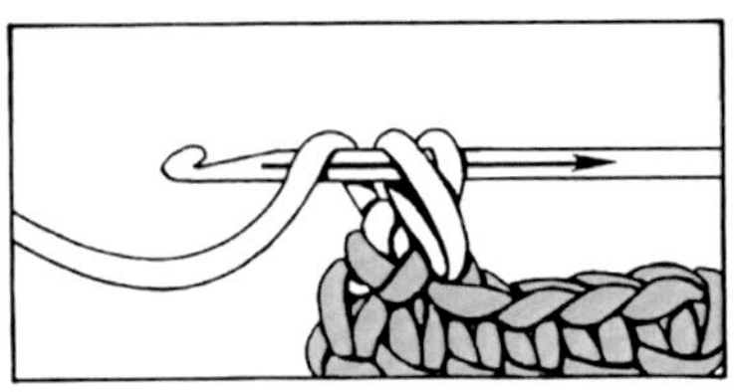

Fig. 11d

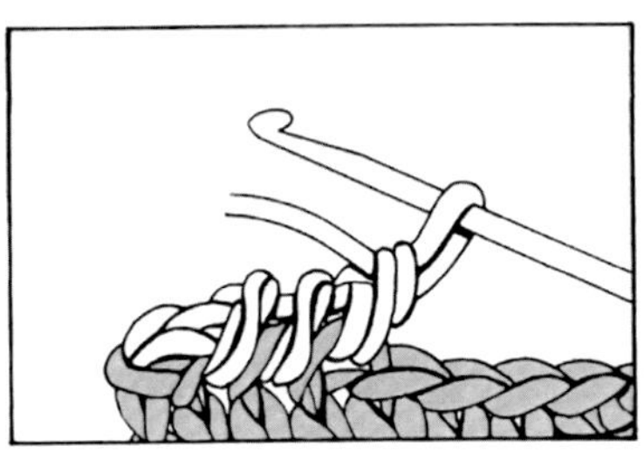

Row 3: Working in unused loop of prev row (behind Knurl sts), sc in first sc and in each sc across; ch 1, turn.

Row 4: Sc in next sc and in each sc across, ending by working last sc in turning ch; ch 1, turn.

POPCORN STITCH *(abbreviated PC)*

Fig. 12

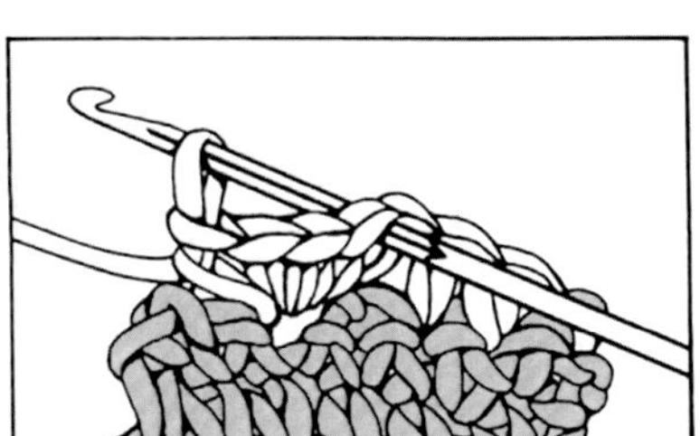

Work 4 sc into same st, drop loop from hook, insert hook into first sc of 4-sc group, hook dropped loop and pull through, ch 1 to close **(Popcorn made)**.

FISHERMAN POPCORN STITCH *(abbreviated FPC)*

– multiple of 4 plus 1 st, 4 rows. Use larger hook.

Row 1: Working into prev row of sc, sc in next sc, ★ ch 1, skip next sc, work PC in next sc ***(Fig. 12)***, ch 1, skip next sc, sc in next sc; rep from ★ across, do **not** work in turning ch; ch 1, turn.

Row 2: Working loosely, sc in first ch-1 sp, ★ ch 1, sc in next ch-1 sp; rep from ★ across; ch 1, turn.

Row 3: Work PC in first ch-1 sp, ★ ch 1, sc in next ch-1 sp, ch 1, work PC in next ch-1 sp; rep from ★ across, ending by working PC in turning ch; ch 1, turn.

Row 4: Rep Row 2.

Row 5: Sc in first ch-1 sp, ★ ch 1, work PC in next ch-1 sp, ch 1, sc in next ch-1 sp; rep from ★ across, ending by working sc in turning ch; ch 1, turn.

Repeat Rows 2-5 for pattern.

Finishing Row: Work 2 sc in each ch-1 sp across, ending by working 2 sc in turning ch; ch 1, turn.

FRONT AND BACK POST STITCH

Fig. 13

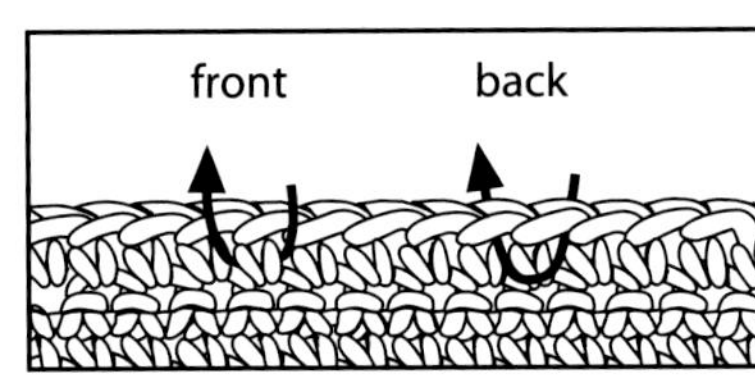

Work appropriate post stitch in row or rows below, in front of, or behind stitch indicated.

DIAMOND PATTERN – multiple of 6 plus 1 st, 8 rows.

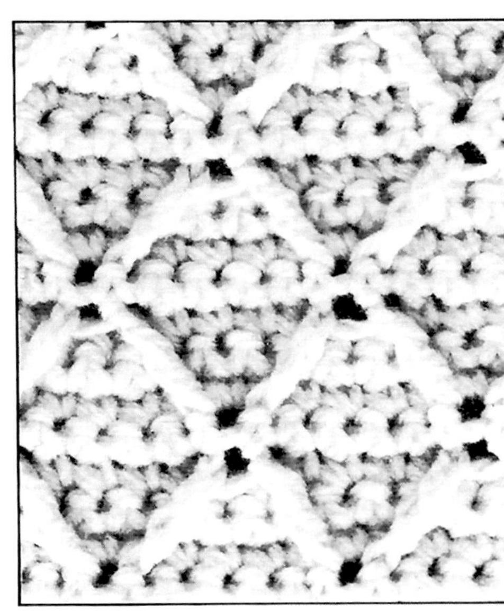

Note: On this pattern, beg rows with sc in sc at base of turning ch (first sc); do **not** work final sc in turning ch.

Row 1: Working into prev row of sc, sc in first sc and in each sc across, ending by working last sc in last sc of prev row; ch 1, turn.

Rows 2 and 3: Rep Row 1.

Row 4: Sc in each of first 2 sc, working from **front *(Fig. 13, page 14)***, tr around 2nd sc on Row 1 (3rd row **below**), skip next 4 sc on Row 1, tr around next sc on Row 1, ★ skip next 2 sc, sc in each of next 4 sc, tr around sc next to last tr, skip next 4 sc on Row 1, tr around next sc on Row 1; rep from ★ across, skip next 2 sc, end by working sc in each of last 3 sc; ch 1, turn.

Rows 5-7: Rep Rows 1-3.

Row 8: Work tr around sc **above** first tr of Row 4 (3rd row **below**), skip first sc, ★ work sc in each of next 4 sc, tr around sc next to last tr, skip next 4 sc on Row 5, tr around next sc, skip next 2 sc; rep from ★ across, ending by working tr around sc next to last tr, skip next sc, sc in last 2 sc; ch 1, turn.

POPCORN DIAMOND – multiple of 8 plus 2 sts, 10 rows.

Row 1: Working into prev row of sc, sc in each of next 4 sc, ★ work 4 sc in next sc, pull up loop, drop loop, insert hook in first sc of 4-sc group ***(Fig. 12, page 14)*** pull dropped loop through, ch 1 to close **(Popcorn made) *(abbreviated PC)***, sc in each of next 7 sc; rep from ★ across, ending by working sc in each of rem 4 sc and in turning ch; ch 1, turn.

Row 2: Sc in each sc and PC across, ending by working sc in turning ch; ch 1, turn.

Row 3: Sc in each of next 2 sc, ★ work PC in next sc, sc in each of next 3 sc; rep from ★ across, ending by working sc in each of rem 2 sc and in turning ch; ch 1, turn.

Row 4: Rep Row 2.

Row 5: Sc in next sc, ★ work PC in next sc, sc in each of next 5 sc, work PC in next sc, sc in next sc; rep from ★ across, ending by working sc in last sc and in turning ch; ch 1, turn.

Row 6: Rep Row 2.

Row 7: Rep Row 3.

Row 8: Rep Row 2.

Row 9: Rep Row 1.

Row 10: Rep Row 2.

CABLE STITCH – multiple of 3 plus 1 st, 2 rows.

Row 1: Working into prev row of sc, sc in next sc, ch 3, skip next 2 sc, sc in next sc ***(Fig. 14a)***, **turn**, sc in each ch just completed ***(Fig. 14b)***, sl st in next sc (sc **before** ch was begun) ***(Fig. 14c)***, **turn**, working **behind** ch-3, sc in each of 2 skipped sc ***(Fig. 14d)***, ★ ch 3, skip st where prev ch was attached and next 2 sc, sc in next sc, **turn**, sc in each ch just completed, sl st in sc where prev ch was attached, **turn**, working **behind** ch-3, sc in each of 2 skipped sc; rep from ★ across, ending by working sc in turning ch; ch 1, turn.

Fig. 14a

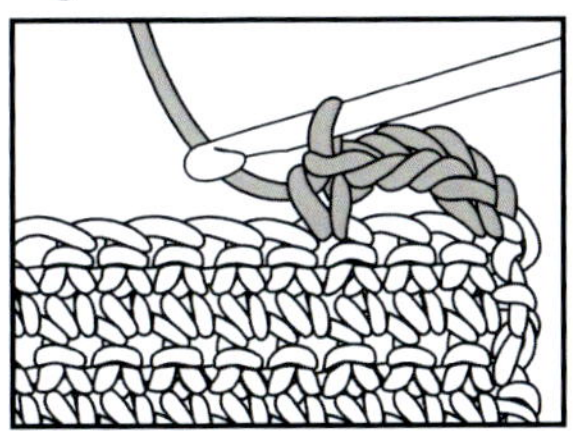

Fig. 14b

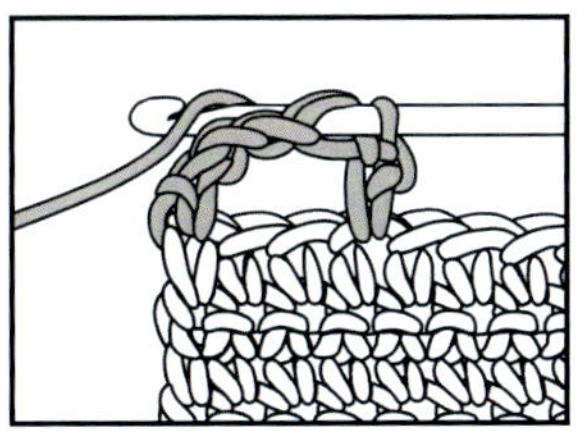

Fig. 14c

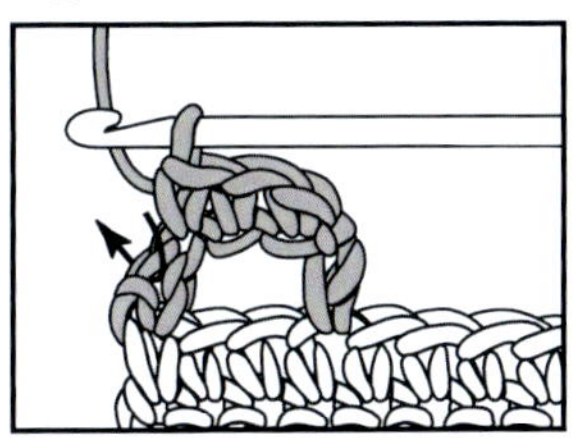

Fig. 14d

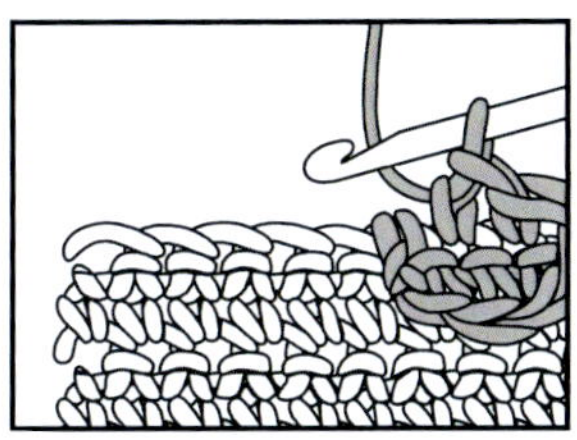

Row 2: Skip first sc, ★ work 2 sc in next sc (**behind** cable), sc in next sc (**behind same** cable), skip sc where ch was attached on prev row; rep from ★ across, ending by working 2 sc in turning ch; ch 1, turn.

Show us what you're working on!

Share your project photos with us on social media.
Tag us @leisureartsinc or use #leisurearts